Deer mice go out at night.

1

They look for seeds and
fruit. A ripe strawberry is
a treat!

Deer mice also watch
for danger.

A hungry owl may swoop
down with sharp claws!

You can find a deer
mouse's home under a tree
or a rock.

Bark and moss make the
home warm and cozy.

Deer mice have babies
at least four times a year.

The babies grow up fast.
In just one season, they are
on their own.